Startup Dot Comms

By Yvan Goudard

First Edition: 2024

ISBN: 9798227692061

Disclaimer: This is a work of non-fiction. While the author has made every effort to ensure the accuracy and completeness of the information contained in this book, he assumes no responsibility for errors or omissions. Any slights of people or organizations are unintentional. The author used AI-powered tools for proofreading and editing this book.

To all the startup founders I've met over the years—Your passion, resilience, and vision to change the world inspire me daily. This book is for you. Keep striving, keep innovating, and keep pushing the boundaries of what's possible.

Prologue

Think about the last time you were in a room full of excited entrepreneurs pitching their ideas. Everyone's passionate, determined, and has a product or service they truly believe in. But as you listen to pitch after pitch, something becomes clear: the startups that rise above the rest aren't necessarily the ones with the most innovative products—they're the ones that know how to communicate.

Poor communication kills the best ideas. In a fast-moving world, it's not enough to have a breakthrough product or a disruptive business model. Your ability to communicate effectively—whether with your team, your customers, your investors, or the public—will make the difference between success and failure.

In the early days of any startup, communication often feels easy. There's a small team, everyone's on the same page, and you have direct contact with everyone involved. But as you start to grow, complexity creeps in. Miscommunications begin to happen, investors need more detailed updates, your customer base expands, and suddenly, what was once simple becomes chaos.

This book isn't just about how to pitch to investors or write a well-crafted email to your clients. It's about mastering the art of communication across all facets of your startup—internally and externally. Whether you're building trust with a new partner, leading a team, or crafting a brand message that resonates, your communication skills will determine how far your startup can go.

The startups that succeed aren't just the ones with the best products—they're the ones that communicate their vision, inspire action, and build lasting relationships. Let's explore how you can do the same.

Introduction - the Power of Communication in Startups

S tartups move fast. Every day, founders and teams make quick decisions, change priorities, and adapt to shifting markets. In this fast-paced world, communication isn't just a tool—it's the foundation of everything.

Why is communication so crucial in startups? Because at every stage, from idea to execution, you're interacting with people. You're rallying your team around a shared vision. You're convincing investors that your product can change the world. You're persuading customers that you're the best solution for their needs. At the heart of every one of these interactions is communication.

Think of communication as the backbone of your startup. Without it, things fall apart. Your team becomes misaligned, your investors lose confidence, and your customers look elsewhere. But when communication is strong, it becomes the fuel that drives innovation, builds trust, and accelerates growth.

This book isn't just a guide to pitching or public speaking—it's a comprehensive roadmap for mastering communication at every level of your business. And when you get communication right, everything else follows.

In the upcoming chapters, you'll learn:

- How to build a culture of open, transparent communication within your team.
- The art of crafting the perfect investor pitch, backed by data and a compelling story.
- How to communicate authentically with your customers, turning them into loyal advocates.
- The role of mentors, advisors, and angel investors in shaping your startup's journey.
- How to handle the media, tell your story effectively, and handle crises transparently.

No matter what stage your startup is in, one thing remains constant: communication is fundamental. And this book will help you master it.

Let's get started.

Chapter 1 - the Internal Engine – Communication Within the Startup Team

Startups are intense. They move at a pace that can feel overwhelming. If communication isn't tight, everything spirals out of control. You might have the best product or service in the world, but if your team doesn't communicate well, all this won't matter. It's not just about speaking—it's about making sure people hear, understand, and act on the same information.

Every startup begins with a vision, usually crystal clear in the founder's mind. But the challenge is getting it out of his head and into everyone else's. This is where most startups stumble. When the vision isn't shared effectively, people start working on different objectives, with conflicting priorities, and this ends up in chaos. In some cases, that chaos leads to burnout or even failure.

Think about how Google started. Larry Page and Sergey Brin weren't just building a search engine—they were on a mission to organize the world's information. Sure, they began in a garage like many startups, but that mission was repeated so often that everyone, from the first engineer to the marketing team, knew exactly what they were working toward. It wasn't just about the search algorithm; it was about the bigger picture.

As a founder, you're not just telling people what the product is—you're painting a picture of why it matters. Repetition is key. You might feel like a broken record, but trust me, if you're not repeating it, people aren't hearing it enough. You need to be relentless in pushing your vision because if you don't, people will fill in the gaps with their own interpretations, and that's when things start falling apart.

"If you're not tired of repeating your vision, you're not saying it enough."

Let me say it again:

"If you're not tired of repeating your vision, you're not saying it enough."

Openness as a Foundation

But vision alone isn't enough. It needs to sit within a culture of openness. If people are afraid to speak up or challenge ideas, your startup will never grow. There's a fine line between being decisive as a founder and creating an environment where people feel their voices are heard.

Take Basecamp, for example. They decided early on to avoid standing meetings as they often stifle creativity and add pressure. Instead, they created a culture where people can take their time to think, write out responses, and engage in deeper conversations. There's no rush to jump to a conclusion on the spot. It gives people space to think —and space to innovate.

And that's the key: innovation happens when people feel safe contributing their ideas without fear of being shut down. If your team feels like their opinions matter, they'll contribute more. If they feel like speaking up could make them look foolish or, worse, put their job at risk, they'll stay silent. And that silence will cost you.

You, as a founder, need to create a space where it's okay to disagree. Some of the best ideas come out of heated, passionate debates. But here's the trick— make sure it's about the ideas, not the people. Disagreement should always be respectful and focused on making the product or service better, not tearing anyone down.

Tools for Communication

As your startup grows, communication needs to evolve. In the early days, when it's just a handful of people, communication is easy. You're all in the same room, talking constantly. But as the team expands, you need systems in place. That's where tools like Slack, Notion, or Zoom come in.

But don't fall into the trap of thinking more tools mean better communication. In fact, too many tools can lead to confusion and overwhelm. Your team will end up spending more time checking notifications than actually working. The key is to find the right balance.

Buffer, for instance, operates fully remotely with a globally distributed team. They use Slack for real-time communication but have strict guidelines to prevent burnout—no one is expected to reply after hours, and long discussions are reserved for asynchronous, thoughtful conversations. Their transparency is also built into the system. They don't just use these tools to share tasks; they use them to share company goals, progress, and even setbacks. Everyone knows what's happening, all the time.

As your team grows, these tools should support communication, not replace it. Make sure that people still talk, brainstorm, and share ideas. It's easy to hide behind a screen and send messages all day, but startups need real conversations to thrive.

Practical Advice:
- Slack for quick updates, but with clear boundaries (no one should feel the need to respond instantly).
- Notion for tracking projects and shared knowledge.
- Zoom for face-to-face interaction, but only when necessary.

Striking the Balance Between Over-Communication and Silence

One of the hardest things to master as a founder is figuring out how much to communicate. It's a balancing act—you don't want to overwhelm people with constant updates, but you also don't want to leave them in the dark. Over-communicating can feel like micromanaging, while under-communicating creates confusion and distrust. So where's the sweet spot?

The answer lies in transparency. Be open about the big things—your vision, your goals, the company's financial health. When people have context, they make better decisions. But don't micromanage the small stuff. Trust your team to handle the day-to-day tasks once they understand the broader goals.

Tobi Lütke, the CEO of Shopify, is famous for his transparency. He openly shares the company's long-term strategy with his employees, so they know exactly where they're headed. This level of openness builds trust and empowers his team to make decisions without constantly needing approval.

And let's talk about meetings. In startups, meetings can easily become the biggest time sink. Amazon's two-pizza rule is a great example of how to keep things lean—if a meeting needs more than two pizzas to feed the group, it's too big. Keep meetings small and focused. Better yet, avoid them unless absolutely necessary. Written updates or short check-ins can save time and keep people productive.

Handling Conflict

Now, what about conflict? It's inevitable. No matter how well you communicate, there will be disagreements. And that's a positive thing. Healthy conflict pushes the company forward. It forces people to challenge assumptions, look at problems from different angles, and come up with better solutions. But there's a difference between productive conflict and destructive conflict.

Netflix has a unique "culture of candor." Employees are encouraged to give direct feedback, even to the CEO. This level of honesty might seem uncomfortable, but it creates a culture of trust. When people know they can speak their mind without fear of repercussions, the team moves faster, and the company benefits.

The key to navigating conflict is to keep it focused on the problem, not the people. When things get personal, communication breaks down. But when everyone is focused on the same goal—making the product better—the debate becomes constructive.

A startup's internal engine runs on communication, and if you get it right, everything else falls into place.

Next up: Pitching your startup to investors—how to tell a story that gets them on board.

Chapter 2 - Pitch Perfect – Communicating With Investors and VCs

Raising money for your startup feels like a high-stakes game. You're not just selling your product, you're selling a dream—a dream that may not even be fully formed yet. It's easy to think investors care only about the numbers, the spreadsheets, and the graphs, but the truth is that they care about the story you tell. Data is vital, but it's the narrative that hooks them.

The key to nailing your pitch isn't just about perfecting slides. It's about weaving together a story that makes investors believe in your vision as much as you do. The challenge? You've got just minutes—maybe even seconds—to capture their attention, which means clarity and confidence are everything.

Start with the Problem, Not the Product

One of the biggest mistakes founders make in their pitch is diving straight into the product. You're passionate about it, and you've likely spent every waking moment refining it, so it's natural to want to showcase it. But here's the thing—investors don't care about your product. At least, not at first. They care about the problem you're solving.

Look at Airbnb's original pitch. They didn't jump into how their platform worked. Instead, they focused on the problem: hotel prices were too high, and travelers wanted a cheaper, more local experience. That's what caught investors' attention. It wasn't until they understood the problem that they were ready to hear about the product.

When you start with the problem, you set the stage. You show investors that you understand the market, the pain points, and the opportunity. The product? It's just the solution. But the problem has to come first.

> **Tip:** Don't just say, "People are paying too much for X." Paint a picture. Help them feel the pain of the problem. Make them want a solution before you even mention that you have one.

Your Story is the Data

Once you've laid out the problem, it's time to show how your product solves it. This is where the data comes in, but here's the trick—data alone isn't enough. You need to turn that data into a story. How does your product solve the problem in a way that no one else can? What do your early users say? How does the market react to your solution?

Think of it like this: data without context is just numbers. It's your job to make those numbers meaningful. Let's say you've got 1,000 active users. That number by itself isn't impressive. But if you explain that you gained those users in just two months with zero marketing spend, now the story becomes compelling. Investors start to see the potential behind the numbers.

In the early days of Stripe, their pitch wasn't just about processing payments. Their pitch was about how they made something as complex as payments simple for developers. They didn't just throw out numbers—they showed how they were solving a huge pain point for a specific audience. And because they framed the data in the context of that story, it made investors care about the numbers.

> **Example**: If you're pitching to investors, don't just throw out numbers like "We've grown 50% this quarter." Instead, frame it: "We've grown 50% this quarter with a team of just three people and no marketing budget. Imagine what we could do with your investment."

The Investor's Perspective: What They're Really Listening For

Here's the thing—investors have heard a thousand pitches. They've seen the same slides, the same growth charts, and the same promises of disruption. So how do you stand out? You speak their language. Investors care about a few core things, and if you hit these points clearly and concisely, you've already won half the battle.

- **Market Size**: Investors want to know if the problem you're solving is big enough. They're looking for scale. If your solution only works for a tiny niche, it's not going to grab their attention. So when you talk about your market, make sure you're showing how your solution fits into a larger trend or growing demand.

- **Traction**: It's not just about your product being great; it's about whether or not people are actually using it. Investors want to see proof that there's interest, even if it's in the early stages. Customer testimonials, early sales, or user engagement metrics all help paint a picture of traction.

- **Team**: More than anything, investors are betting on you and your team. They're asking themselves, "Can these founders execute? Do they have the grit to stick it out when things get tough?" Show them why your team is uniquely qualified to solve this problem.

- **The Ask**: Be clear about what you need and what it will accomplish. Investors don't want to guess. If you're asking for $500,000, explain exactly how that will help you reach your next milestone.

Key Insight: Speak directly to these concerns. Investors are busy, and they don't have time to decode a vague pitch. Be clear, concise, and confident.

Managing the Data Room: Transparency Builds Trust

Once you've captured their interest with your pitch, they'll want to dig deeper into the numbers. This is where the data room comes in—a place where investors can see all the gritty details. Think of it like your startup's financial and operational diary. It needs to be organized, accurate, and transparent.

Investors appreciate founders who don't try to gloss over the rough spots. If there's a weak spot in your financials or projections, be upfront about it. Explain why it exists and what you're doing to address it. This builds trust. Investors aren't expecting perfection—they're expecting honesty.

> **Example**: WeWork's downfall is a classic example of what happens when transparency breaks down. They sold a vision that didn't match the reality of their financial situation. When investors finally got a look inside, the trust was gone, and the funding dried up.

Transparency in your data room is your opportunity to build long-term relationships. When investors see that you're willing to show both the good and the bad, they'll be more inclined to trust you with their money.

The Art of Managing Expectations

Let's say you've secured the initial interest from investors. You're in the follow-up meetings, things are going well, and they're ready to make an offer. It's easy to get carried away here, to promise the moon in hopes of securing the investment. But over-promising is a dangerous game.

Investors don't expect your startup to go from zero to unicorn in a year. What they do expect is that you'll hit the milestones you lay out in your pitch. The best way to build trust with investors is to set realistic expectations and then exceed them. Under-promise and over-deliver.

> **Example:** Amazon is a company that's consistently managed investor expectations well. Jeff Bezos famously told early shareholders not to expect profits for years. Instead, he promised long-term growth, and he delivered exactly that.

The key to managing investor relationships is the same as any relationship: honesty and clarity. Tell them what to expect, keep them updated, and deliver on your promises. They're investing in you for the long haul, and building trust from the start is what will keep them on board when times get tough.

Investors don't just want numbers; they want a story, a vision, and a team they can believe in.

Next up: Now that you've won over investors, it's time to focus on your external audience—communicating your brand's message to clients and the market

Chapter 3 - Building the Brand – External Communication With Clients and the Market

Your startup might have the best product on the market, but if your external communication doesn't resonate, no one will care. Brand communication isn't just about logos or catchy slogans. It's about how you make people feel, how you connect with them emotionally, and how you show up in their lives. Whether you're talking to clients, potential customers, or the broader market, every message you send shapes your reputation.

Message Over Mechanics

Many startups fall into the trap of focusing too much on how they communicate—investing time in designing beautiful websites, posting on every social media platform, or crafting the perfect email template. While all of these things matter, what matters more is what you're saying. The most polished pitch or beautifully designed email will fall flat if your message doesn't resonate with your audience.

Think about Apple. For years, their tagline was "Think Different." It wasn't about the technology. It was about what that technology made possible. They weren't selling iPhones—they were selling creativity, freedom, and innovation. The message was clear: This is for people who want to change the world. And that's what people bought into.

Tip: Strip your message down to its essence. What are you really trying to say? Focus on one core idea and repeat it everywhere—on your website, in your pitches, even in casual conversations. Consistency is what turns a message into a brand.

Consistency is Key, but Authenticity is Critical

Consistency is important, but here's the thing—people can tell when you're faking it. If your brand message sounds polished but feels hollow, your audience will disconnect. Customers today, especially Millenials and Gen Z, can spot inauthenticity a mile away: they won't buy in if you're trying to sound like something you're not.

"People don't buy what you do; they buy why you do it." – Simon Sinek.

It's not enough to just have a catchy brand message. You have to believe in it. Every person on your team has to embody it. If your company is about sustainability, it's not just about posting a few eco-friendly messages on Instagram—it's about ensuring your supply chain reflects those values. If your brand is about customer service, everyone, from the CEO to the newest intern, should live and breathe that commitment.

> **Tip**: Look inward before you communicate outward. Make sure your brand message aligns with your internal values and culture. Authenticity comes from within.

Telling a Story, Not Selling a Product

The best way to communicate your brand is through storytelling. People don't remember features and specs; they remember stories. Stories are how we connect as humans, and they're how brands connect with audiences.

When Patagonia talks about its products, it doesn't just say, "Our jackets are waterproof." They tell you about the founder's adventures in the wild, the environmental impact of production, and the people who craft each item. They take you on a journey. That's what makes you care.

> **Tip**: Think about the story behind your startup. Why did you start it? What problem are you solving, and for whom? Then, think about your customers' stories. What does your product enable them to do? Use stories to bring your brand to life.

Know Your Audience: Speak Their Language

One of the most critical elements of external communication is knowing who you're talking to. Clients, customers, and the general market don't all speak the same language. It is totally different to communicate with a B2B client than it is to talk to a casual consumer.

Start by defining your audience. Is your customer base primarily tech-savvy millennials? Small business owners? Corporate executives? Each group has different expectations, and how you present your brand needs to reflect that.

Take Slack as an example. In its early days, Slack didn't market itself as just a messaging tool for teams. It positioned itself as the solution for teams who wanted to work better together. The used a language void of tech jargon—it was simple, human, and focused on improving collaboration. That resonated with both small startups and larger enterprises because they tailored their messaging to different types of teams.

> **Tip:** Adjust your tone and messaging based on your audience, but always stay true to your core brand voice. Whether you're writing a formal proposal for a client or a fun social media post, the essence of your brand should always shine through.

Visual Identity Speaks Louder Than You Think

Words matter, but so does the way things look. Your visual identity is a significant part of how people perceive your brand, often before they even read your messaging. The colors, fonts, and imagery you choose create an immediate impression. Are you playful and creative? Serious and professional? Your visuals need to match the message you're putting out there.

Take Dropbox's visual overhaul a few years ago. They shifted from a minimalist design to a more vibrant and creative look. Why? Because they wanted to be seen as more than just file storage—they wanted to be a creative solution for teams and individuals. Their new look reflected that shift in how they wanted to be perceived.

Handling Public Relations (PR) Like a Pro

When it comes to managing how the public perceives your brand, PR is your best friend—or worst enemy. Good PR can launch your brand into the spotlight, while bad PR can tear it down overnight. In today's hyper-connected world, one misstep can spread like wildfire, so how you communicate during good times and bad is critical.

When crises arise, transparency is your most powerful tool. Trying to sweep mistakes under the rug or sidestep responsibility will backfire. Customers appreciate honesty, and they'll forgive you if you own up to mistakes and communicate openly about how you're fixing them. Just look at how Tylenol handled its crisis in the 1980s—when faced with a product tampering scandal, they immediately pulled products off the shelves and communicated clearly with the public. That transparency saved the brand.

Beyond Customers – Building a Community

Good communication doesn't just attract customers—it builds a community. You're not just trying to sell a product; you're trying to create loyal advocates who believe in what you do. Brands like Nike and Apple don't just have customers—they have fans. These people wear their logos proudly, defend them online, and promote their products without being asked.

Building a community starts by listening. Engage with your audience. Social media is more than a broadcast channel—it's a two-way street. Respond to comments, ask for feedback, and let your customers feel they're part of your brand story.

"Your brand is what people say about you when you're not in the room." – Jeff Bezos.

Your brand isn't just what you say—it's what people hear, feel, and remember.

Next up: We'll explore how to effectively communicate with partners and suppliers, creating relationships that drive your startup forward.

Chapter 4 - the Art of Pitch Decks – Aligning Your Story With Data

Every founder knows the importance of the pitch deck. It's the window into your startup—the tool that can open doors to investment, partnerships, and new opportunities. But here's where many stumble: they think the pitch deck is about impressing people with numbers, charts, and projections. In reality, your pitch deck is a storytelling device.

The best pitch decks don't just present data—they weave data into a compelling narrative. They paint a picture that makes the audience believe in your startup's potential and trust that you're the team to execute the vision. So, let's talk about how to turn a collection of slides into a powerful story that sticks.

Simplicity Wins. Every. Single. Time

First things first: simplicity. The more information you cram into your pitch deck, the more you lose your audience. Investors aren't interested in reading lengthy text blocks or analyzing every financial figure in your spreadsheets. They want clarity. They want to understand your business model, the problem you're solving, and why your solution is better—all in a matter of minutes.

This doesn't mean you need to dumb things down. In fact, simplifying complex ideas takes skill. The goal is to distill your entire pitch into a clear, easy-to-follow narrative that gets 's attention. Keep your slides clean—minimal text, simple visuals, and big ideas.

"If you can't explain it simply, you don't understand it well enough." – Albert Einstein.

The hardest part of preparing a pitch deck is cutting out everything that feels important but ultimately clutters your story. It's about getting to the essence of what matters. When Airbnb pitched their idea, their early deck had just 10 slides. They didn't overload it with excessive data or financial forecasts—they got to the heart of the problem they were solving and why their solution mattered.

Visuals Speak Louder Than Numbers

Your pitch deck is a visual tool. Investors will remember images and charts more than dense paragraphs of text. So, make sure your visuals tell the story just as much as your words do. A single well-designed graph can speak volumes about your growth trajectory. A chart that shows a clear upward trend will stick in your mind far longer than a list of bullet points outlining your progress.

But here's the key—don't use visuals just for the sake of using them. Each image, graph, or infographic needs to serve a purpose. It should advance the story you're telling. If a visual doesn't reinforce your core message, leave it out.

Take a look at Stripe's early pitch deck, which used just a few simple slides and clear visuals to highlight the pain points developers faced when integrating payment systems. They didn't need a lot of fluff. They just needed to show that they understood the problem better than anyone else and that their solution made integration radically simpler.

> **Tip**: Use visuals to show, not tell. A well-placed graph or diagram can explain a complicated process in seconds, far more effectively than a paragraph of text ever could.

The Flow: Building Momentum Through the Deck

Think of your pitch deck as a journey. You're taking your audience from problem awareness to excitement about your solution. If your slides don't flow well, you'll lose that momentum. Every slide should build on the previous one, taking your audience deeper into your story. This is where structure becomes critical.

1. **Start with the problem:** Remind your audience why they should care. What's broken? What's the pain point? Make them feel it.

2. **Introduce your solution:** Now that you've got them thinking about the problem, hit them with your solution. What's unique about your approach? Why are you the right team to solve this?

3. **Show the market opportunity:** No matter how brilliant your solution is, it won't matter unless the market is big enough. Show your audience the size of the opportunity. Where's the demand?

4. **Traction and validation:** Have you already gotten some early wins? What milestones have you hit? This is where data comes in—use it to back up your claims.

5. **The business model:** How do you make money? Be clear and direct. Investors want to know how you'll turn a profit.

6. **The team:** Investors often invest in people, not just ideas. Show why your team is uniquely qualified to execute the vision. Highlight key team members and their expertise.

7. **The ask:** Finally, be explicit about what you need. How much money are you raising, and what will you use it for?

This is a simplified version of what a deck should communicate, and it will vary based on the stage of your startup, but you get the idea.

Tying Data to the Narrative

It's easy to throw numbers onto slides and hope they impress. But numbers alone aren't enough. The magic happens when you tie your data to the narrative you're building. Think of data as proof points, supporting the claims you're making throughout the pitch.

For example, when talking about your traction, don't just list numbers: "We've grown 300% in six months." Instead, weave it into your story: "In just six months, with no marketing spend, we've grown 300%—purely from word-of-mouth. Imagine what we could achieve with your backing."

Data is most powerful when it's part of the story. It provides the credibility your audience needs to trust that you can deliver. But on its own, data is just noise.

Handling Tough Questions: Be Honest and Prepared

Here's a scenario you'll face in every pitch meeting: the tough questions. Investors will poke holes in your projections, challenge your assumptions, and ask about your weaknesses. It's tempting to overinflate numbers or sidestep concerns, but the best way to handle these questions is with transparency.

If an investor asks about a weak spot in your financials or a competitive threat, don't dance around it. Acknowledge it and explain how you're addressing it. Investors aren't looking for perfection—they're looking for honesty and realism. They know no startup is flawless, but they want to see how you think on your feet and how you handle challenges.

> **Tip**: Prepare for the tough questions before you walk into the room. Know where your weaknesses are and have a clear, thoughtful response ready.

The Secret to a Good "Ask"

When it's time to ask for money, be clear. Many founders fumble this part, either by being too vague

("We're raising funds") or too aggressive ("We need $2 million and we'll dominate the market!"). Your "ask" needs to be specific, grounded in realistic expectations, and focused on what it will enable you to achieve.

Instead of saying, "We're raising $1 million," say, "We're raising $1 million to hit three key milestones: launch our beta product, hire two additional engineers, and secure 10,000 new users. This will position us for a Series A within the next 18 months."

Be clear about what the investment will do for your company and what the investor can expect in return. When you tie your ask to specific goals, it feels more tangible and less risky.

A great pitch deck isn't about overwhelming your audience with data—it's about crafting a clear, simple, and compelling story that shows why your startup matters.

Next up: Now, let's explore how to build strong communication with suppliers and partners— relationships that will help you scale effectively.

Chapter 5 - Navigating Relationships – Communication With Suppliers and Partners

A startup isn't an island. It relies on a web of relationships to thrive—partners, suppliers, service providers. These external relationships can make or break your ability to scale. Often, startups focus so much on customers and investors that they neglect these critical partnerships. But here's the truth: how you communicate with your suppliers and partners could be the difference between success and stagnation.

Building strong relationships with partners and suppliers isn't just about negotiating the best price or signing contracts. It's about creating long-term partnerships built on trust, transparency, and alignment of goals. These are the people and companies that will fuel your growth, so your communication with them must be clear, consistent, and mutually beneficial.

Clarity from Day One

The foundation of any strong relationship is clarity. When working with suppliers or partners, you need to communicate your needs, expectations, and timelines clearly from the very start. If you're vague about what you want, you'll end up with missed deadlines, supply chain issues, and endless back-and-forths.

Set the tone early by being direct. What do you need? When do you need it? And how will success be measured? Don't assume that the other party will automatically understand what's most important to you—they have their own business and priorities, too.

> **Tip**: At the beginning of any partnership, set up a clear communication plan. This could be as simple as a weekly check-in or a shared project management tool, but the key is to ensure everyone stays on the same page.

Alignment of Values

It's easy to choose a supplier based on cost or convenience. But here's the thing: long-term partnerships are about more than just getting the best deal. If your values don't align with those of your partners or suppliers, you'll run into problems down the road.

Let's say you're building a brand around sustainability, but your supplier cuts corners when it comes to environmental practices. That'll to create friction—not just in your relationship with them, but in your ability to stay true to your brand values.

Startups often face tough decisions when balancing cost with values, but remember that a misaligned supplier can hurt more than your budget—they can hurt your brand's integrity. Find partners who share your vision and commitment, whether that's about quality, sustainability, or innovation.

The Power of Transparency

Transparency in communication is non-negotiable when it's about building trust with suppliers and partners. Whether you're expecting a delay in payment or foresee challenges in meeting a contractual obligation, let them know as soon as possible. Surprises in business are rarely pleasant.

Imagine you're running into cash flow issues and won't be able to pay your supplier on time. The worst thing you can do is stay silent until the last minute. Instead, be upfront about the situation and propose a plan for when they can expect payment. Most suppliers appreciate honesty and will be more likely to work with you if you're transparent, rather than springing bad news on them at the eleventh hour.

> **Tip:** Be as open about your challenges as you are open about your successes. If something goes wrong, share it immediately and focus on a solution together.

Negotiation Isn't a Battle

Too many founders think of negotiations as a win-lose situation: if they get a better price, they've won; if they've had to compromise, they've lost. Negotiation should be about finding a solution where both parties walk away happy. It's not about squeezing every last penny out of your supplier, but rather building a relationship that's sustainable for both sides.

Successful negotiations are about creating a balance where both sides feel like they're benefiting. If your supplier feels like they're constantly getting the short end of the stick, they'll either deprioritize your business or, worse, start cutting corners on quality.

> **Example**: Look at companies like Toyota, which famously cultivated long-term relationships with their suppliers by focusing on mutual benefit. Instead of pushing for rock-bottom prices, they worked closely with suppliers to improve efficiency and quality, creating a stronger, more reliable supply chain.

Long-Term Vision vs. Short-Term Gains

One of the mistakes startups make is focusing too much on short-term gains when negotiating with suppliers or partners. You might save a few dollars in the short term by switching suppliers or pushing for deep discounts, but if that relationship breaks down in a year, the costs of finding a new partner could outweigh the savings.

Think long-term. Your goal should be to create partnerships that can grow with your business. This means not only thinking about your current needs but also anticipating your future ones. As your startup scales, you'll need partners and suppliers who can scale with you.

For example, if you're launching a new product, don't just think about your first production run. Will your supplier be able to handle an increase in volume if demand spikes? Do they have the flexibility to accommodate changes in your needs as you grow? These are the kinds of questions you should be asking.

Communicate Your Growth Plan

Suppliers and partners aren't just there to provide a service—they can be key players in your growth. The more they understand your long-term vision, the better they can serve your needs. Keep them in the loop about your growth plans, new product launches, or strategic pivots.

Tip: Invite key suppliers and partners into your business planning. If they understand where you're headed, they can align their resources and priorities to better support your growth.

By building a more collaborative relationship, you give them the opportunity to anticipate your needs and be proactive in offering solutions. This also strengthens the relationship, as they feel like a true partner rather than just a service provider.

When Things Go Wrong

No matter how well you plan, things will go wrong. Orders will be delayed, shipments will get lost, or miscommunications will happen. The true test of any partnership is how both parties respond when things don't go as planned.

If your supplier fails to meet a deadline, avoid jumping straight to blame. Instead, approach the situation as a shared problem that needs solving. This mindset will keep the relationship intact while addressing the issue at hand. Ask: What went wrong? How can we prevent it from happening again? What can both sides do differently?

Example: In 2010, after the Icelandic volcano eruption disrupted global shipping routes, many businesses faced delays in receiving goods. Some companies lashed out at their suppliers, while others worked collaboratively to find alternative shipping routes or temporary solutions. Those who treated the issue as a shared challenge ended up with stronger relationships.

Appreciation Goes a Long Way

It's easy to get caught up in the transactional nature of business relationships, but suppliers and partners are people, too. A simple "thank you" or recognition of their efforts can go a long way. When you appreciate their hard work and dedication, they're more likely to go above and beyond for your startup.

Whether it's a handwritten note after a big order is delivered, a small present for the holidays, or simply an acknowledgment in your emails, showing appreciation can turn a good relationship into a great one.

Tip: Don't just communicate when there's a problem or when you need something. Regularly check in with your partners and suppliers, and show that you value the relationship beyond the transactions.

Your startup's success hinges on the relationships you develop with suppliers and partners—treat them as true collaborators, not just service providers.

Next up: In the next chapter, we'll dive into the art of customer-centric communication—how to build loyalty and engagement by listening and responding to your audience.

Chapter 6 - Clients, Customers, and Community – Communicating for Retention

The true challenge for a startup isn't just acquiring customers—it's keeping them. Customer retention is where long-term growth and profitability live. In fact, a 5% increase in customer retention can increase profits by 25% to 95%, depending on the industry. Retention isn't only about delivering a great product; it's about creating meaningful, ongoing communication with your customers. We will explore how to turn first-time buyers into loyal advocates, using thoughtful, customer-centric communication.

Customer-Centricity: Listen Before You Talk

Most companies, especially in their early stages, are focused on getting their message out. They spend endless energy crafting the perfect email campaigns, optimizing social media posts, and figuring out how to push their product. But great communication with customers isn't about how well you talk—it's about how well you listen.

Startups often forget that the most valuable feedback comes directly from the people using the product. When was the last time you actively listened to what your customers were saying—without filtering their input through your own lens? The best customer communication strategies start with listening.

> **Tip:** Implement regular customer feedback loops—surveys, user interviews, and open communication channels like social media and direct email. These channels are goldmines for understanding what customers need and how your startup can improve. Don't just collect data—act on it.

> **Example:** Slack, in its early days, grew its product by listening intently to user feedback. Instead of assuming they knew what users wanted, they invited feedback, rapidly iterated based on that input, and built features that responded directly to customer needs. That active listening fueled their rapid growth.

The Power of Personalization

Personalized communication is no longer a luxury in customer retention—it's an expectation. Generic, one-size-fits-all messaging doesn't work in a world where customers expect tailored experiences. Studies show that 80% of consumers are more prone to purchase from a company that provides personalized experiences. But personalization goes beyond simply inserting a customer's name into an email.

True personalization means understanding where your customers are in their journey, what they've bought or shown interest in, and how you can provide them value at each stage. It's about making every interaction feel relevant, timely, and thoughtful.

Tip: Use customer data not just to target, but to enrich the customer experience. Segment your audience based on behavior, past purchases, or engagement levels. When you send an email, it shouldn't just have their name at the top—it should speak to their specific needs, challenges, or preferences.

Building a Community, Not Just a Customer Base

Retention isn't just about getting customers to return for repeat purchases—it's about creating a sense of belonging. People want to be part of something bigger than themselves. They want to feel connected to a community, not just a brand. This is where the concept of community-driven brands comes into play.

Look at brands like Glossier. From the start, they understood that building a community of loyal fans would set them apart from traditional beauty brands. They created open channels for customers to give input on product development, and they treated their customer base as co-creators. This sense of ownership turned customers into advocates, who were not only repeat buyers but evangelists for the brand.

Handling Complaints: Turning Problems into Opportunities

No matter how good your product or service is, complaints will happen. It's inevitable. And the way you handle those complaints can either damage your brand or strengthen it. Too often, companies see complaints as negative feedback that needs to be minimized or avoided. However, complaints are actually opportunities to create loyal customers.

When a customer takes the time to share a problem or dissatisfaction, they're giving you a second chance. If you respond swiftly, empathetically, and effectively, you can turn a disgruntled customer into a lifelong advocate. In fact, studies show that customers who have a positive resolution to their complaints are more loyal than those who've never had a problem in the first place.

"A complaint is a gift." – Janelle Barlow and Claus Møller.

Instead of viewing complaints as burdens, treat them as valuable insights into where your product, service, or communication may need improvement. It's about showing your customers that you care, not just about selling a product, but about their experience and satisfaction.

> **Tip:** Train your customer support team not just to solve problems, but to listen empathetically. The tone and approach in resolving an issue can make all the difference in whether the customer feels valued or dismissed.

Consistency Across Channels

In a multi-channel world, customers interact with your brand in more ways than ever before—through social media, emails, your website, and in-person experiences. Inconsistency across these touchpoints can create confusion and frustration, especially if the customer experiences conflicting messages or levels of service.

For example, imagine a customer receiving excellent support via chat but feeling ignored on social media. That inconsistency damages trust because it shows a lack of coordination and care. Every touchpoint—whether it's a tweet, a support email, or an in-app message—should reflect the same tone, level of service, and brand values.

> **Tip:** Create clear communication guidelines for your team, outlining the tone and style that should be used across all platforms. Regularly audit your communication channels to ensure consistency and identify gaps.

Customer Loyalty Programs: Communication in Action

A well-structured loyalty program isn't just about points and rewards—it's an ongoing dialogue between your brand and your most valuable customers. Loyalty programs provide an excellent platform for personalized communication. Every interaction within the program is an opportunity to thank your customers, surprise them, or offer them something of value.

But too many loyalty programs feel transactional—customers accumulate points, redeem rewards, and the relationship ends there. To truly build loyalty, your communication around the program needs to feel special. It's about recognizing milestones, acknowledging birthdays or anniversaries, and offering personalized perks.

> **Example**: Starbucks' loyalty program doesn't just reward purchases—it creates a personalized experience by offering tailored rewards based on purchasing behavior. Whether it's a free drink on their birthday or bonus points during specific times, customers feel like the program is designed for them, not just everyone.

Tip: Use your loyalty program to nurture a deeper relationship with your top customers. Don't just rely on generic emails—offer exclusive content, early access to new products, or personalized offers that make your customers feel like VIPs.

Proactive Communication: Stay Top of Mind

Customer retention isn't just about responding to problems—it's about staying on your customers' radar even when there's no immediate transaction. This is where proactive communication comes in. By regularly engaging your customers with valuable, relevant content, you keep them engaged with your brand even between purchases.

The mistake many companies make is overloading their customers with sales emails. Instead, focus on offering real value. This could be useful tips, insider content, or updates on how you're evolving the product to better meet their needs.

Tip: Use email as a tool for engagement, not just sales. Share stories about your team, behind-the-scenes updates on product development, or customer success stories. Keep your communication human, authentic, and customer-focused.

Loyalty is a Two-Way Street

The most important thing to remember about customer retention is that loyalty isn't something you can demand or assume—it's something you earn. Every interaction, every email, every tweet is an opportunity to build trust, deepen the relationship, and show your customers that you value them beyond their wallets.

Customers who feel valued will be more inclined to stick around, even if competitors offer lower prices or newer features. They'll forgive mistakes, offer feedback, and, most importantly, they'll spread the word. But they'll only do that if they feel truly connected to your brand.

Communication isn't just about transactions—it's about creating lasting relationships with your customers by listening, engaging, and showing them they matter.

Next up: In the next chapter, we'll explore the role of mentors and advisors—how to foster open communication with those who guide your startup's growth.

Chapter 7 - Mentors, Advisors, and Angels – Learning Through Feedback

Every founder needs help. The idea that successful entrepreneurs are lone wolves, hacking their way to the top with nothing but grit and determination, is a myth. In reality, building a startup requires a network of experienced people who can guide you, offer feedback, and challenge your thinking. Enter mentors, advisors, and angel investors —the external voices that can shape the trajectory of your company, if you know how to communicate with them effectively.

But here's the catch: not all feedback is created equal. Learning from these key relationships means not only listening but also understanding how to interpret, filter, and act on the advice you receive.

Mentorship: Beyond Advice, It's About Perspective

Mentors play a crucial role in any founder's journey. They're not just there to give advice; they offer a new perspective—one that comes from years of experience, successes, and mistakes. The right mentor can help you see blind spots, avoid common pitfalls, and accelerate your growth by focusing your efforts.

But here's something to remember: mentors aren't there to make decisions for you. Their role is to ask the hard questions, challenge your assumptions, and guide you toward thinking critically about your choices. Too many founders look to mentors for answers, when in fact, the most valuable mentors are the ones who push you to find the answers yourself.

> **Tip:** When communicating with a mentor, ask questions that invite deeper thinking. Instead of asking, "What should I do?" ask, "What would you consider if you were in my position?" or "What questions should I be asking myself here?"

Example: In his early days at LinkedIn, Reid Hoffman had several mentors who didn't tell him what to do but helped him frame key strategic decisions by pointing out the bigger picture. Instead of offering step-by-step instructions, they asked questions that forced Hoffman to think critically about market positioning and long-term vision. This type of mentorship allowed LinkedIn to pivot from its original idea of networking for work-related tasks to the massive professional platform it became.

Advisors: Structured Guidance and Accountability

Advisors differ from mentors because they are typically more formal and structured in their roles. While mentors offer informal advice and wisdom, advisors usually have specific areas of expertise that align with your startup's needs—marketing, technology, scaling operations, or financial strategy. Advisors are more hands-on, providing tactical input and helping you navigate specific challenges.

Effective communication with your advisors starts with clarity. You need to be upfront about what you expect from the relationship. Are you seeking strategic advice on growth? Do you need help with product-market fit? Or are you looking for someone to hold you accountable to your milestones?

The biggest mistake startups make is not being specific enough with their advisors. Vague or directionless conversations won't yield actionable results. To maximize the value of your advisors, give them context and clear objectives to focus on. They should know where you need help, what challenges you're facing, and how their input will drive action.

> **Tip:** Create a cadence of regular communication with your advisors, whether monthly check-ins or quarterly reviews. Send a brief agenda before each meeting to ensure that the discussion stays focused on the most pressing issues.

Angels: Balancing Support and Feedback

Angel investors bring more than money to the table —they bring experience, connections, and often, feedback, occupying a unique space in the startup ecosystem. As early-stage investors, they're taking a high risk on you and your vision. This means their feedback can sometimes be more direct, while it's also tied to their vested interest in your success.

Angel investors want to see progress, but they also want transparency. One of the most valuable things you can do as a founder is maintain clear and open communication with your angels. Regular updates, both good and bad, build trust. Too often, founders wait until they've reached a major milestone to share progress, but angels want to be part of the journey, not just the destination.

"We don't expect perfection, but we do expect honesty. If things are tough, tell us. If you're seeing great results, celebrate with us. We're in this together." – A common sentiment from early-stage investors.

Angels also offer feedback, often drawing from their experiences with the different startups they've invested in. But here's the challenge: sometimes that feedback is shaped by what worked for different companies and may not align perfectly with your vision. That's why it's essential to listen carefully but not blindly follow every suggestion.

Tip: When angels give you feedback, ask follow-up questions to understand the reasoning behind their suggestions. Feedback ingrained in past experiences is valuable, but it's up to you to determine whether it fits your unique situation.

Filtering Feedback: Not Every Piece of Advice Is Actionable

With so many external voices—mentors, advisors, angels—it's easy to feel overwhelmed. One of the toughest skills a founder must develop is learning how to screen feedback. Not every piece of advice, no matter how well-intentioned or experienced the source, is right for your startup.

Here's the reality: mentors and advisors predominantly speak from their own perspective, shaped by their own experiences. What worked for their company or their industry may not apply to yours. It's your job to listen carefully, consider the context of their feedback, and decide what aligns with your vision and goals.

Tip: After receiving feedback, give yourself time to process it. Don't feel pressured to act on advice immediately. Reflect on how it fits into the broader picture of your startup and use it to inform your decision-making, not dictate it.

Example: Dropbox co-founder Drew Houston sought advice from various mentors and investors, many of whom had different perspectives on how to scale the business. Some advised him to focus on enterprise clients, while others pushed for a consumer-first approach. Houston took time to process the feedback and ultimately blended both strategies, creating a product that appealed to individual users and companies alike.

Establishing Trust and Transparency

The foundation of any successful relationship—whether with a mentor, advisor, or angel—is trust. And trust is built through transparency. As a founder, it's tempting to present only the good news when communicating with these stakeholders. However, the most valuable feedback often comes from discussing the challenges, roadblocks, and uncertainties.

If your startup is struggling to hit a growth target or facing unexpected obstacles, share that with your mentors and advisors. These are the moments when their feedback and guidance can have the most impact. Sugarcoating or hiding the truth will only lead to frustration on both sides.

> **Tip**: Be transparent in your updates, especially when things aren't going according to plan. Your mentors and advisors are there to help you navigate the tough times, not just celebrate the wins.

Learning to Let Go: When to Part Ways

Not every mentor or advisor will be the right fit for the long haul. As your startup evolves, so will your needs. The mentor who helped you get your first MVP out the door might not be the right person to guide you through scaling. The advisor with deep expertise in early-stage fundraising might not have the operational knowledge you need as you expand.

Recognizing when a relationship has run its course isn't a failure—it's a sign of growth. It's important to communicate openly when you feel the dynamic needs to shift. Sometimes it means transitioning an advisor to a less active role or finding new mentors who can bring fresh perspectives to your current challenges.

> **Tip**: Regularly reassess the value of your mentor and advisor relationships. Are they still providing the insights and guidance you need at this stage? If not, it's time to seek new voices.

Learning through feedback is an art, not a science. It's about listening, filtering, and knowing when to act. The key is to build trust and transparency with the people who guide you while staying true to your own vision.

Next up: Let's explore the art of media and public relations—how to shape the narrative about your startup in the public eye.

Chapter 8 - Navigating Media and Public Relations – Shaping the Narrative

In the digital age, your startup's public image can spread faster than ever before. One tweet, one blog post, or one news article can set the tone for how your brand is perceived. While this speed can be a powerful tool, it also makes navigating media and public relations (PR) a delicate balance. You're no longer just communicating with your customers or investors—you're communicating with the world.

Effective media relations aren't just about getting press. They're about shaping your startup's story in a way that builds trust, attracts customers, and influences stakeholders. From proactive storytelling to handling crises, mastering the art of media and PR can be one of the most impactful tools in your startup's arsenal.

Telling Your Story: Controlling the Narrative Before It Controls You

When it comes to media and public relations, the most important principle is this: if you don't control your story, someone else will. Startups often make the mistake of letting their story evolve passively, allowing the media, competitors, or even disgruntled customers to shape their public image. But in today's media landscape, you need to be proactive.

Your story isn't just a summary of what your product does—it's about why you exist, the problem you're solving, and the impact you want to make. And the sooner you start telling that story, the better. Media outlets, bloggers, influencers, and even potential customers are looking for more than just products—they want to understand the mission and vision behind your startup.

Take Warby Parker, for example. They weren't just selling affordable glasses—they positioned themselves as a company that challenged the high-cost eyewear industry while giving back through their "buy a pair, give a pair" initiative. This simple, clear story resonated with the media, customers, and investors alike. It wasn't just about glasses—it was about revolutionizing an industry and making a difference.

> **Tip:** Start with a clear, simple narrative. Answer three key questions: What problem are you solving? Why does it matter? How is your approach different from others?

Building Relationships with the Media

Media relationships, like all relationships, are built on trust. Journalists and bloggers receive hundreds of pitches a day, many of which are irrelevant, impersonal, or self-promotional. To stand out, your approach has to be thoughtful and authentic. But even more important than securing a one-time media hit is developing long-term relationships with key journalists and publications that cover your industry.

Tip: Don't wait for a big announcement to start building media relationships. Reach out to journalists before you need something from them. Share insights, offer commentary on industry trends, or simply introduce yourself and your startup's mission.

One mistake startups often make is pitching their product or story to the wrong journalists. Before you send that press release or email, take the time to understand which reporters cover your industry, which publications matter most to your audience, and what kind of stories they tend to cover. Journalists appreciate when startups do their homework, and it increases the likelihood that your story will be picked up.

Example: Look at how companies like Spotify strategically built relationships with tech and lifestyle media outlets long before they became a household name. They didn't rely on one-time coverage but cultivated ongoing conversations with journalists, positioning themselves as thought leaders in both music and technology.

Crafting the Perfect Pitch

Getting media attention is about more than having a great product—it's about framing that product in a way that makes it newsworthy. This is where many startups struggle. They assume that just because they're doing something innovative, the media will care. But in reality, you need to craft your story in a way that captures attention.

Start by thinking like a journalist. What's in it for their readers? What makes your story timely, relevant, or surprising? Media outlets want stories that inform, entertain, or solve a problem for their audience. It's your job to show them how your startup fits into that framework.

Tip: When pitching your story, focus on the bigger picture, not just the product. Is there a trend you're part of? A larger societal shift you're responding to? Make it clear why your story matters now.

Example: When Peloton started pitching to the media, they didn't just talk about their high-tech fitness equipment. They framed it as part of the broader trend of at-home fitness and the rise of digital wellness communities. By positioning themselves within a growing trend, they made their story more compelling to journalists and readers alike.

Navigating a PR Crisis: Transparency and Speed Are Everything

No startup is immune to crises. Whether it's a product failure, a data breach, or a customer backlash, the question isn't if a crisis will happen—it's when. The good news is that how you respond can actually strengthen your brand if handled correctly. The key? Transparency and speed.

The worst thing you can do in a PR crisis is go silent. Customers and the media are looking for answers, and if you don't provide them, they'll fill in the gaps with their own narratives. Immediate, clear communication is critical to maintaining trust. Even if you don't have all the answers yet, acknowledge the issue, explain what steps you're taking, and commit to providing updates as soon as you have more information.

"A crisis is an opportunity riding the dangerous wind." – Chinese Proverb.

Look at how JetBlue handled its PR crisis in 2007 when severe winter storms left passengers stranded for hours. Instead of deflecting blame or minimizing the issue, JetBlue's CEO made a public apology, explaining what went wrong and laying out specific steps the company would take to prevent it from happening again. That transparency turned a potential disaster into an opportunity to rebuild trust with customers.

Leveraging Social Media: More Than Just Marketing

Social media has revolutionized how startups interact with the public. It's not just a marketing tool —it's a direct line of communication with your audience. Whether you're responding to a customer complaint, sharing behind-the-scenes updates, or launching a new product, social media gives you the chance to shape your narrative in real time.

But with that opportunity comes responsibility. Your social media channels are a reflection of your brand, and every tweet, post, or comment shapes how people perceive you. Inconsistent messaging, tone-deaf responses, or failure to engage with your audience can quickly damage your reputation.

For example, brands like Wendy's have built a strong social media presence not just by promoting their products but by engaging in witty, sometimes irreverent conversations with their audience. This humanizes their brand and creates a sense of connection, making them more than just another fast-food chain.

PR Isn't One-Size-Fits-All

It's important to remember that PR isn't just about media coverage. It encompasses every interaction your startup has with the public, from interviews and blog posts to social media and customer support. Startups need to view PR as an ongoing dialogue with the world, not a one-time effort to secure a headline.

Consider brands like Tesla. Their PR strategy isn't reliant on traditional media coverage—in fact, Tesla famously does very little paid marketing or PR. Instead, they focus on creating newsworthy moments, generating buzz through product launches, CEO commentary, and social media engagement. This approach keeps Tesla in the headlines without following the conventional rules of PR.

Staying Consistent Across Channels

One of the biggest challenges for startups is maintaining consistency across all the various platforms and channels they use to communicate with the public. From your website to your social media profiles, press releases, and blog posts, your messaging should be cohesive. Inconsistent communication not only confuses customers but also weakens your brand identity.

> **Tip:** Create a brand messaging guide that outlines your key messages, tone of voice, and the core story you want to tell. Share this guide with your entire team to ensure everyone is on the same page.

PR is about more than just media coverage—it's about telling your story, building relationships, and handling challenges with transparency and speed.

Next up: In the final chapter, we'll bring everything together—how communication can help your startup thrive, scale, and create a lasting impact.

Chapter 9 - Keeping It All Together – Developing a Communication Strategy for Growth

By now, you've seen how every facet of your startup depends on effective communication—whether it's with your team, your investors, your customers, or the media. But what happens as your startup grows? The challenge of scaling doesn't just apply to your product or operations—it applies to your communication strategy, too.

Growth creates complexity. More people, more customers, more stakeholders mean more communication—and with that, more chances for miscommunication. The secret to managing this complexity is having a well-defined communication strategy that scales alongside your company.

Scaling Communication: The Foundation of Consistency

When you're a small team, communication is simple. You can have a quick chat with everyone involved, decisions happen fast, and everyone's aligned. But as your startup grows, keeping that clarity and alignment becomes more difficult. That's why a scalable communication strategy is essential.

Tip: Document your communication processes early. Whether it's how your team collaborates, how you update investors, or how you engage customers, writing down these processes ensures that everyone knows the "how" as you grow. This will prevent confusion and save time as new team members and stakeholders come on board.

As you add layers of management and more team members, your communication processes should evolve to include new tools and structured updates. But that doesn't mean you lose the simplicity. The goal is to scale communication without adding unnecessary complexity.

Maintaining Clarity During Growth

The biggest risk for a growing startup is losing clarity. It's easy to drown in information—long email threads, countless Slack messages, back-to-back meetings—until no one knows what the priority is anymore. As you scale, maintaining clarity around goals, vision, and decision-making becomes crucial.

Example: Amazon's famous "working backwards" process ensures clarity across all levels of the company. When planning a new product or feature, teams start by writing a press release and FAQ, focusing on the customer benefits. This forces clarity in thinking and ensures everyone understands the final goal before a single line of code is written.

This principle can be applied to any communication process. Make sure every team member understands the "why" behind every decision or project. The clearer the goals, the less room there is for miscommunication as your company grows.

Building a Culture of Communication

As you scale, communication can't just be a top-down directive—it needs to be part of your company culture. Everyone on your team, from your newest hire to your senior leaders, should feel comfortable communicating openly and effectively. This is especially important in larger teams, where silos can easily form, and information gets lost.

"The way we communicate with others and with ourselves ultimately determines the quality of our lives." – Tony Robbins.

Create spaces where open communication is encouraged, not just between departments, but within them. Encourage your team to ask questions, challenge ideas, and offer feedback. The more communication is part of your culture, the better aligned your team will be, even as you grow.

Communication Across Borders

For many startups, growth means expanding into new markets—often across different regions or countries. This brings a new set of communication challenges, including language barriers, cultural differences, and time zones.

If you're expanding internationally, your communication strategy needs to account for these differences. It's not just about translating materials into different languages; it's about understanding the cultural nuances that shape how people communicate, both internally and externally.

> **Tip:** When expanding into new regions, take the time to understand local communication norms. What works in one culture may not work in another, so adapting your approach to fit regional expectations is crucial for success.

At the same time, keep your core communication values intact. Even as you tailor your messaging for different markets, the essence of your brand and how you communicate your vision should remain consistent. This balance between adaptation and consistency is key to successful cross-border growth.

Leveraging Technology for Seamless Communication

Technology plays a critical role in managing communication as you scale. From Slack to Zoom to Asana, there are countless tools available to streamline team communication, project management, and customer interactions. The trick is choosing the right tools for your stage of growth and ensuring your team uses them effectively.

> **Example**: GitLab, a fully remote company with over 1,300 employees spread across the globe, uses an open and transparent communication strategy supported by technology. Every document, from team updates to meeting notes, is public within the company. This ensures that everyone, regardless of location, has access to the same information. GitLab uses tools like Slack, Zoom, and Google Docs, but the key to their success is having a system that ensures transparency and prevents silos.

When scaling, the goal is to use technology to support communication, not replace it. Tools should make it easier for your team to collaborate, not create additional layers of complexity.

Balancing Efficiency and Engagement

As your company grows, communication can become highly transactional—status updates, progress reports, meeting agendas... But efficient communication isn't the same as engaging communication. Even as you scale, it's important to maintain a human touch in how you communicate with your team, your customers, and your stakeholders.

"Communication leads to community, that is, to understanding, intimacy, and mutual valuing." – Rollo May.

Make sure that communication doesn't become robotic. Personalized interactions, especially with customers and key partners, are what drives loyalty and engagement. Even internally, taking the time to have real conversations with your team—whether in one-on-one check-ins or town hall meetings—can make all the difference in keeping everyone motivated and aligned with the company's mission.

Navigating Growing Pains: Transparency is Key

Growth is exciting, but it also brings growing pains —team members spread thin, deadlines that get missed, or projects that don't go as planned. During these times, transparency becomes your most valuable tool. If your team feels in the dark about decisions, or if your investors feel blindsided by unexpected challenges, trust will erode.

Be upfront about the challenges of growth, whether that's internally with your team or externally with stakeholders. Transparency doesn't mean you have to broadcast every problem, but it does mean being honest about where things stand and what you're doing to address any issues.

> **Tip:** Use regular, transparent updates to keep everyone in the loop, whether it's through internal newsletters, all-hands meetings, or investor reports. When people know what's going on, they're more likely to support you during the inevitable ups and downs of growth..

The Importance of Feedback Loops

One of the most important parts of a growing communication strategy is creating feedback loops.

As your company scales, feedback needs to be a constant, ongoing process. Whether it's feedback from your customers, your employees, or your advisors, these insights help you stay grounded and responsive.

> **Example**: Airbnb is known for its commitment to gathering feedback. They continually seek input from hosts, guests, and employees through surveys, one-on-one interviews, and roundtables. This feedback informs everything from product updates to company culture initiatives. By maintaining open feedback loops, Airbnb stays connected to its community, even as they scale globally.

Building feedback into your communication strategy isn't just about addressing issues—it's about ensuring that your company evolves in response to the needs of the people it serves.

Communication is the foundation on which your startup grows. As you scale, your communication strategy must evolve to ensure clarity, transparency, and engagement at every level.

Startups thrive on the strength of their communication. Whether it's internally with your team or externally with your customers and partners, keeping communication clear, open, and adaptable will be the key to your success.

Conclusion - Communication as Your Startup's Superpower

By now, it should be clear that communication isn't just a skill—it's your startup's superpower. From day one to scaling into a thriving business, every success and every failure can be traced back to how well you've communicated with your team, your customers, your investors, and the market at large.

The startups that grow, innovate, and leave a lasting impact are the ones that understand communication is more than sending messages—it's about building relationships, creating alignment, and inspiring action. It's about knowing when to listen, when to speak, and how to adapt as your business evolves.

As you look to the future, think of communication as your constant. No matter what changes—a new market opportunity, a fresh wave of competition, or an internal pivot—your ability to clearly articulate your vision, navigate challenges, and foster connection will determine your success.

Here are the most important takeaways to carry
forward:

- Internal communication is the foundation of
  everything. A team that communicates openly and
  transparently will move faster, solve problems
  better, and stay aligned with your vision. Your
  culture starts with how you communicate.

- Investors care about the story you tell. Numbers
  matter, but it's the narrative that gets them on
  board. Be clear, be compelling, and show them why
  your startup is the one to bet on.

- Your customers are your best advocates. By
  communicating with them in a way that feels
  personal, authentic, and consistent, you'll build a
  community that supports your growth, even when
  the going gets tough.

- Mentors, advisors, and angels are not just sources
  of feedback—they're partners in your journey. Stay
  transparent, be open to learning, and know when
  to act on their advice.

- The media can make or break you. Control your
  story before others do, and when crises arise,
  handle them with honesty and speed. Transparency
  builds trust, and trust sustains your brand.

As your startup grows, communication will become
more complex, but it should never become an
afterthought. If anything, it becomes more critical.
Keep your lines of communication open, your
message clear, and your vision front and center.

Success in the startup world isn't just about having
the best product or the best idea—it's about how well

you connect with people, how you inspire them to believe in your vision, and how you lead them to act.

So as you move forward, remember: Communication isn't just a tool—it's your advantage. Use it wisely, and your startup won't just survive—it will thrive.

Glossary

Angel Investors

Individual investors who provide capital for startups, typically in exchange for ownership equity or convertible debt. Angel investors often offer more than just money—they also provide advice, industry connections, and mentorship.

Brand Messaging

The central narrative a company uses to communicate its value proposition, mission, and identity to its customers. This includes the tone, language, and key messages used in marketing, advertising, and customer interactions.

Clarity

In the context of communication, clarity refers to the quality of being clear and easy to understand. It involves eliminating confusion and ensuring that all parties have the same understanding of a message or objective.

Communication Channels

The methods or platforms used to convey messages between individuals or groups. Examples include emails, meetings, Slack, social media, and media outlets.

Crisis Communication

A strategy for communicating with stakeholders during times of crisis, such as product failures, PR disasters, or unexpected disruptions. It involves transparency, quick responses, and clear messaging to manage public perception and maintain trust.

Customer-Centric Communication

A communication approach that focuses on understanding and addressing the needs, preferences, and behaviors of customers. It involves listening to feedback, personalizing interactions, and creating meaningful relationships with customers.

Data Room

A secure space (often virtual) where startups share critical company data, financials, and documentation with potential investors during the due diligence phase of fundraising.

Elevator Pitch

A concise, persuasive presentation of your startup or idea that can be delivered in the time it takes to ride an elevator—typically 30 seconds to 2 minutes. The goal is to spark interest and invite further conversation.

Feedback Loops

A communication process in which feedback from customers, employees, or stakeholders is continuously collected, reviewed, and used to improve processes, products, or strategies.

Investor Pitch

A formal presentation or conversation where a startup founder or team presents their business idea, growth potential, and funding needs to investors to secure financial investment.

Mentors

Experienced professionals who offer informal guidance, advice, and perspective to startup founders, often helping them navigate strategic decisions and personal growth challenges.

Pitch Deck

A presentation, often in slide format, is used to communicate a startup's business model, value proposition, market opportunity, financials, and team to potential investors or partners.

PR (Public Relations)

The practice of managing and shaping the public image of a company through communication strategies, media relations, and handling crises. Effective PR ensures that a company's message aligns with its goals and resonates with its audience.

Scalable Communication

Communication strategies and processes that are designed to grow and adapt alongside a company, ensuring that information remains clear, accessible, and effective as the organization expands.

Stakeholders

Individuals or groups with a vested interest in a company's performance and decisions. In startups, stakeholders include founders, investors, employees, customers, suppliers, and sometimes the public.

Storytelling

The use of narrative to communicate key messages in a way that is engaging, memorable, and impactful. In startups, storytelling is often used in pitches, branding, and customer engagement to connect emotionally with the audience.

Sustainability (in partnerships)

The practice of building long-term, mutually beneficial relationships with suppliers, partners, and stakeholders that are designed to last, ensuring steady growth without compromising trust or values.

Transparency

The practice of openly sharing relevant information, challenges, and successes with stakeholders, both internally and externally. Transparency builds trust and helps maintain strong relationships.

Traction

A term used to describe measurable progress or momentum that a startup has achieved. This could be in the form of user growth, revenue generation, or market penetration—indicators that validate the startup's potential.

Value Proposition

A clear statement that explains what benefits a company's product or service provides, how it solves customer problems, and why it is better than competing solutions. It is a key part of a startup's messaging strategy.

Vision

A startup's long-term goal or mission. It's the broader purpose or future state that the company is working toward, often serving as the guiding principle for decision-making and communication.

References

1. **Godin, Seth** – *Linchpin: Are You Indispensable?* Penguin Books, 2010.

    Seth Godin's work influenced the style of this book, particularly the focus on individual creativity, leadership, and communication.

2. **Godin, Seth** – *This Is Marketing: You Can't Be Seen Until You Learn to See.* Penguin Books, 2018.

    A valuable resource on marketing and communication, emphasizing clarity and emotional connection with customers.

3. **Ries, Eric** – *The Lean Startup: How Today's Entrepreneurs Use Continuous Innovation to Create Radically Successful Businesses.* Crown Business, 2011.

    Provides the foundational principles of how startups should iterate quickly and communicate both internally and with stakeholders, including investors and customers.

4. **Hoffman, Reid, and Yeh, Chris** – *Blitzscaling: The Lightning-Fast Path to Building Massively Valuable Companies.* Crown Business, 2018.

This book offers insight into how startups scale, including the importance of communication with investors and stakeholders during periods of hypergrowth.

5. **Blank, Steve** – *The Startup Owner's Manual: The Step-by-Step Guide for Building a Great Company.* K&S Ranch Press, 2012.

A guide for founders navigating communication with investors, teams, and customers, touching on both internal alignment and external messaging.

6. **Barlow, Janelle, and Møller, Claus** – *A Complaint Is a Gift: Using Customer Feedback as a Strategic Tool.* Berrett-Koehler Publishers, 1996.

This book offers a deep dive into how to turn customer complaints into opportunities for communication and growth, influencing the section on customer retention and problem-solving.

7. **Campbell, Bill** – *Trillion Dollar Coach: The Leadership Playbook of Silicon Valley's Bill Campbell.* Harper Business, 2019.

A key reference for understanding the role of mentors and advisors in startup success, emphasizing transparency and communication.

8. **Goleman, Daniel** – *Emotional Intelligence: Why It Can Matter More Than IQ.* Bantam Books, 1995.

Emotional intelligence plays a key role in how founders communicate with teams, investors, and customers, touching on empathy, transparency, and leadership communication.

9. **Sinek, Simon** – *Start with Why: How Great Leaders Inspire Everyone to Take Action.* Penguin Books, 2009.

This book heavily influences the communication strategy around clarifying and consistently communicating a startup's vision and mission, especially in investor relations.

10. *JetBlue Airways Case Study* – Varied sources analyzing JetBlue's handling of its 2007 PR crisis, where transparency and accountability became key elements of their recovery.

Used as an example of crisis communication done well, with transparency leading to regained customer trust.

11. *Tylenol Crisis Case Study* – Varied sources analyzing Johnson & Johnson's handling of the Tylenol product tampering case in the 1980s, a benchmark for effective crisis communication and public relations management.

Referenced for crisis communication strategies, especially transparency and speed of response.

12. *Buffer Transparency Project* – The Transparency Project: How We Run a Fully Distributed Company. Buffer Blog, various articles.

Buffer's radical transparency in how they communicate internally and externally, particularly around remote work and decision-making processes.

13. *Airbnb Case Study* – Various sources exploring how Airbnb's early growth was driven by active communication with users, as well as how they pivoted based on customer feedback.

Referenced for its use of customer-centric feedback loops and community building.

14. *Patagonia Case Study* – Various sources analyzing Patagonia's use of sustainability messaging and storytelling to create a strong brand community and maintain customer loyalty.

Used to illustrate authentic, values-driven communication with communication with customers.

15. *Peloton Case Study* – Various sources analyzing Peloton's early growth and media strategy, which positioned them as part of a broader wellness and at-home fitness trend.

Referenced for its strategic use of PR and narrative shaping.

Referenced Quotes

1. **"If you're not tired of repeating your vision, you're not saying it enough."**
Source: Yvan Goudard – *(Extensively used in brand-building sessions).*

2. **"People don't buy what you do; they buy why you do it."**
Source: Simon Sinek – *Start with Why: How Great Leaders Inspire Everyone to Take Action*. Penguin Books, 2009.

3. **"Your brand is what people say about you when you're not in the room."**
Source: Attributed to Jeff Bezos
(Commonly referenced in brand-building literature and business leadership discussions).

4. **"Your supply chain is only as strong as its weakest link."**
Source: *Expression commonly used in risk management and logistics.*

5. **"A complaint is a gift."**
Source: Janelle Barlow and Claus Møller – *A Complaint Is a Gift: Using Customer Feedback as a Strategic Tool*. Berrett-Koehler Publishers, 1996.

6. **"We don't expect perfection, but we do expect honesty. If things are tough, tell us. If you're seeing**

great results, celebrate with us. We're in this together."
Source: Common investor sentiment, often discussed in startup and investor relations.

7. **"The best mentors help you outgrow them. They don't hold on too tightly."**
Source: Bill Campbell, discussed in *Trillion Dollar Coach: The Leadership Playbook of Silicon Valley's Bill Campbell.* Harper Business, 2019.

8. **"A crisis is an opportunity riding the dangerous wind."**
Source: *This Chinese proverb is widely used in crisis communication contexts.*

9. **"The way we communicate with others and with ourselves ultimately determines the quality of our lives."**
Source: Tony Robbins – *Awaken the Giant Within.* Free Press, 1991.

10. **"Communication leads to community, that is, to understanding, intimacy, and mutual valuing."**
Source: Rollo May. – *Communication for Business Success*, M Library Publishing, 2010

About the Author

Yvan Goudard is a seasoned branding and communications expert with a passion for storytelling and a deep understanding of the startup ecosystem.

With decades of experience helping brands craft compelling narratives, Yvan has worked with founders and teams to align their vision with messages that drive growth and engagement.

A thought leader and writer who frequently reports on tech and startup events across Southeast Asia, Yvan offers insights into emerging trends and the future of business communication.

His work bridges the gap between technical innovation and human connection, making him a trusted advisor to entrepreneurs navigating the complexities of growth.

Stay Connected!

Thank you for reading *Startup dot Comms: The Communication Blueprint for Startups*. If you found value in the insights shared here, I'd love to stay connected and continue the conversation.

You can follow me on LinkedIn and Medium, where I regularly share thoughts on communication, branding, startups, and the latest trends in the tech ecosystem.

Join me on LinkedIn:
https://linkedin.com/in/yvancgoudard/

Follow me on Medium:
https://medium.com/@y-consulting

I look forward to connecting with you and hearing your thoughts!